OXFORDSHIRE
COUNTRY RECIPES

COMPILED BY
ANN GOMAR

GW00371670

ℛℛ
RAVETTE BOOKS

Published by Ravette Books Limited
3 Glenside Estate, Star Road
Partridge Green, Horsham,
Sussex RH13 8RA
(0403) 710392

Production: Oval Projects Ltd.
Cover design: Jim Wire
Typesetting: Repro-type
Printing & binding: Nørhaven A/S

All recipes are given in Imperial and Metric
weights and measures. Where measurements
are given in 'cups', these are American cups,
holding 8 fluid ounces.

The recipes contained in this book are traditional
and many have been compiled from archival sources.
Every effort has been made to ensure that the recipes
are correct.

RECIPES

CAKES, BREAD and BISCUITS

PRESERVES

OXFORDSHIRE

Oxfordshire is a beautiful county with large areas of fertile agricultural land. It shares borders with six other 'Shires' — Northamptonshire, Warwickshire, Gloucestershire, Wiltshire, Berkshire, and Buckinghamshire. Especially noted for lush pastureland and the production of cereals — corn, barley, oats and wheat — is the area lying in the valley of the upper Thames, and its many tributaries that flow through the county, such as the Cherwell, the Evenlode, the Windrush and the Ock. Watermills and windmills have been a feature of the Oxfordshire landscape for centuries. Over 200 were recorded in the Domesday book, and many can still be seen today.

In the north west rise the Cotswolds, famed for sheep rearing since medieval times. In this lovely region the drystone walls, the cottages — many thatched — manor houses and churches are all built of the local grey limestone or golden ironstone. In the south lie the rolling wooded Chiltern Hills, also an area of sheep rearing and mixed farming.

The rich grass of the famous Vale of the White Horse is excellent for dairy and beef farming, and the production of butter and cheese. The 374-foot long white horse, cut into the chalk on the hillside near the iron age camp of Uffington Castle is said to be more than 2000 years old. At the foot of the hill is an area known as 'The Manger', where legend has it the horse goes to feed. At one time the horse was thought to represent the legendary dragon slain by St. George on nearby Dragon Hill. The Vale of the White Horse used to be famous for producing a delicious cheese, similar to that made in neighbouring Gloucestershire.

Apples from the orchards around Wantage — birthplace in AD 849 of Alfred the Great, whose statue stands in the market place — were often used to make the generous daily cider ration, which was part of the pay for the men working in the corn fields. The cider was taken from the farm to the fields in small hand-barrels of wood or copper. Some of the apple crop was often sent to London on the beautiful Thames sailing barges. Before the development of road transport, sailing barges and the horse-drawn canal boats played a vital part in the transport of goods to and from Oxfordshire.

The rivers have always provided good fishing both for sport and for eating. It is said that during the Middle Ages salmon were so plentiful that they formed a regular part of the poorest person's diet. In modern times a catch of freshwater fish like roach, bream, trout and eels is more likely. Eels from the Abingdon area are renowned for their good quality. Eels were caught with eel spears, slender forks shaped like a hand with metal fingers fixed to a long handle, or in eel traps — long willow baskets baited with rabbit meat. During the Middle Ages the flour mill at Eynsham was owned by the Abbey. The miller paid an annual rent of ten shillings and several hundred eels. Nearby there is still a vehicle toll bridge over the Thames at Cumnor. In earlier times, cattle, sheep and pigs being driven to market in Oxford were also charged from a farthing to a penny per head depending on size. The river banks have always been a popular summer picnic spot, and there is no shortage of attractive riverside pubs offering good food, while spectators at the famous annual Henley Regatta enjoy a full range of out-of-doors eating, from luxury marquee to self catering.

The City of Oxford is divided into the contrasting bustling, commercial 'town' and 'gown' — the 'dreaming spires' of the ancient University. The colleges have splendid dining Halls, and a long history of culinary excellence.

There are many traditions about food in the county, some connected with the University are still carried on today, such as the Boar's Head Ceremony that takes place annually at

Queen's College. When all are seated, including the Provost and Fellows at High Table, the boar's head, with an orange in its mouth, is carried in on a silver dish decorated with rosemary, bay and holly, accompanied by the choir singing the Boar's Head Carol. The Chef places the dish on the table. The orange is presented to the leader of the choir and the rosemary and bay sprigs are distributed among the diners.

Elegant meals would also have been served throughout the centuries at Blenheim Palace, Woodstock, the home of the Dukes of Marlborough and birthplace of Sir Winston Churchill. At Blenheim, an 18th century butter cooler is on view in the Old Palace Dairy. Witney, famous for the manufacture of blankets, has an old Butter Cross, where the women from nearby villages came to sell butter, eggs and cheese. This old charm used to be chanted during butter-making: 'Churn, butter, churn! Come, butter, come! Peter stands at our gate, waiting for a butter-cake. Churn, butter, churn! Come, butter, come! In the former manor at Stanton Harcourt, the home of the Harcourt family for 600 years until the 18th century, the great medieval kitchen can still be seen today. It has huge ovens and a fireplace large enough to roast an ox. Dr. Plot, describing the kitchen, wrote: '... the Fires being made against the Walls and the Smoak climbing up them, without any tunnels or disturbance to the Cooks'. Roasting a whole ox was still popular earlier this century.

The diet of the cottagers in the early 20th century was plain but wholesome. A few chickens and a pig were often kept in the back garden. Most of the pig was skilfully turned into tasty dishes without waste. Children were especially fond of the lard spread on bread, seasoned lightly with salt and pepper, and sometimes sugar. The diet would be supplemented by home grown vegetables and fruit, blackberries from the hedgerows (which women and children also gathered to sell to Frank Cooper's jam factory for ½d.

a pound, after a long walk into Oxford), rabbits, hares, pigeons and even rooks. Henry James Pye, poet laureat to George III, lived in Faringdon House and wrote the nursery rhyme: "When the pie was opened, the birds began to sing, wasn't that a dainty dish to set before the King."

Many traditions also flourished in Oxfordshire villages, and some are still thriving. At the Kirtlington Lamb Ale Festival, the Lord and Lady accompanied by twelve attendants walked in procession with a lamb wearing a blue ribbon round its neck. At Kidlington a lamb was roasted, while Banbury Cakes (made at the Original Banbury Cake Shop) were sold at the local Horse Fair, which attracted visitors from all over the world. Feast Sundays were held in various villages at the end of August or beginning of September. The Bampton in the Bush ceremony, which used to take place at Whitsun but now is on Spring Bank Holiday, consists of a plum cake being carried impaled on a sword, through the village streets accompanied by a fool, fiddler and Morris dancers. This grew from the days when a buck was carried triumphantly back to the village. The villages near the ancient Forest of Wychwood were granted the right to hunt and kill one buck annually in lieu of hunting rights, lost when the forest was claimed by the King for royal hunting alone. Any villagers who touched the sword were given a slice of the buck. Today the legend is that anyone who keeps a slice of the cake for a year, will have twelve months of good luck.

The visitor to beautiful Oxfordshire will find much to see and do, as well as excellent hotels, restaurants and pubs offering an abundance of good food and hospitality.

OXTAIL SOUP

Serves 4

1 lb (450 g) thin end of oxtail
4 oz (100 g) onions, chopped
2 oz (50 g) celery, chopped
8 oz (225 g) carrots, chopped
8 oz (225 g) tomatoes
2 oz (50 g) butter
1½ pints (900ml/ 3¾ cups) brown stock
A pinch of mixed dried herbs
Salt and pepper
2 oz (50 g) flour
2 tablespoons sherry (optional)

Cut the oxtail into small pieces.

Scald, peel and quarter the tomatoes.

Melt 1 oz (25 g) of the butter in a saucepan and fry the vegetables until lightly brown.

Add the stock and herbs.

Season with salt and pepper to taste.

Bring to the boil, cover and simmer gently for up to 4 hours, and at least 2 hours.

Skim off any fat, and remove the oxtail.

Take any meat off the bones, chop and keep it to one side.

Pass the soup through a sieve or blend in a liquidizer.

Melt the remaining butter in a saucepan.

Stir in the flour to make a roux.

Gradually stir in the soup, and bring to the boil, stirring.

Simmer for about 5 minutes.

Add the sherry and chopped oxtail meat.

GREAT AUNT LUCY'S CREAMED
WILD MUSHROOM SOUP

Serves 4

FROM PISHALL FARM

If available, wild mushrooms freshly gathered from the fields give a special flavour to this soup. For many centuries, a warming, nourishing pottage of vegetable soup, served with bread, was the mainstay of most people's diet.

½ lb (225 g) mushrooms
1 onion
3 oz (75 g) butter
¾ pint (450 ml/ 2 cups) chicken stock
2 oz (50 g) flour
¾ pint (450 ml/ 2 cups) milk
Salt and pepper
1 egg yolk
2 tablespoons of double cream
1 whole mushroom for garnish

Wash the mushrooms but do not peel them.

Retain one for garnish.

Roughly chop the mushrooms, using the stalks as well as the caps.

Peel and chop the onion.

Melt half the butter in a saucepan.

Fry the onion until soft but not brown.

Add the mushrooms.

Put the lid on and give the saucepan a good shake to mix the vegetables.

Return to the heat, and cook very gently for 5 minutes.

Gradually add the stock, and simmer for 30 minutes.

Rub the soup through a sieve or blend in a liquidizer.

Melt the rest of the butter in a saucepan.

Stir in the flour.

Gradually add the mushroom stock and the milk.

Bring to the boil, stirring, and cook until the soup thickens.

Season with salt and pepper to taste.

Blend the egg yolk and the cream together.

Add to the soup, and cook for a few minutes without boiling.

Just before serving, slice into four the whole mushroom, including the stalk.

Lay the slices on top of the soup.

This soup is also delicious served chilled.

Mushrooms

TOMATO SOUP

Tomatoes are often called 'love apples'.

1 lb (450 g) ripe tomatoes
1 onion
1 carrot
4 oz (100 g) streaky bacon
2 oz (50 g) butter or margarine
1 dessertspoon tomato purée
1 tablespoon caster sugar
1 pint (600 ml/ 2½ cups) white stock
A pinch of mixed herbs
1½ oz (40 g) flour
2 tablespoons double cream (optional)
Salt and pepper

Chop the tomatoes roughly.

Peel and chop the onion and carrot.

Remove the rind and cut the bacon into small pieces.

Melt the butter in a saucepan.

Add the onion, carrots and bacon and fry gently for about five minutes.

Stir in the flour to make a roux.

Gradually add the stock, stirring, and bring to the boil.

Add the chopped tomatoes, tomato purée, sugar, herbs and seasoning and simmer gently for 30 minutes.

Pass the soup through a sieve or blend in a liquidizer.

Swirl in the cream just before serving, and do not allow the soup to boil again.

Can be served chilled.

HERRINGS IN CIDER

Serves 4

Traditionally herrings are distributed in the village of Clavering at the end of Lent. The cider and herbs give a subtle flavour to this dish.

4 herrings
½ pint (300 ml/ 1¼ cups) cider
½ pint (300 ml/ 1¼ cups) water
1 onion
½ lemon rind, finely grated
4 peppercorns
2 bay leaves
Salt and pepper

Clean the herrings and place them in a casserole dish.

Pour the cider and water over the fish.

Peel and slice the onion.

Add the onion, lemon rind, peppercorns, bay leaves and seasoning.

Cover the casserole, and bake in a moderate oven for 45 minutes to 1 hour, until the fish is tender.

Remove the herrings and arrange them on a serving dish.

Spoon some of the cooking juices over the fish, as required.

Delicious eaten hot or cold.

Oven: 325°F/160°C Gas Mark 3

BONGO BONGO

FROM EXETER COLLEGE

Exeter College, Oxford, originally for men from Devon and Cornwall was founded in 1314 by Walter de Stapledon, Bishop of Exeter, who was murdered for supporting Edward II.

The Hall, built in 1618, was restored after the Battle of Waterloo in 1815. It has a vaulted crypt, and the splendid roof is supported by the carved heads of kings and commoners.

This is a recipe brought to Exeter College many years ago, by a past Fellow from a little restaurant in the back streets of New York. It has come to be associated with High Table, where it is served as a starter.

18 fresh oysters or 1 small can
1 medium onion, chopped
1 clove garlic, crushed
2 tablespoons oil
½ pint (300 ml/ 1¼ cups) single cream
A dash of anchovy essence
A dash of Worcestershire sauce
½ lb (225 g) chopped frozen spinach or
    1 lb (450 g) fresh spinach
1 pint (600 ml/ 2½ cups) vegetable stock
1 tablespoon cornflour (to thicken, if necessary)
Seasoning to taste

Put the oil in a saucepan large enough to accommodate all the ingredients.

Sweat the onion and garlic on a low heat.

Add the chopped spinach (or washed, fresh spinach) and continue to cook until soft.

Meanwhile, boil the oysters in the vegetable stock until cooked.

Then remove six oysters for garnish.

Add the remainder, with the stock, to the saucepan containing the spinach.

Add the remaining ingredients and bring to simmer, then liquidize in a blender.

Return to the heat, adjust the seasoning and thicken with cornflour if necessary.

FRIED EELS

Eels from the Thames are highly rated for flavour.

**2 lbs (900 g) prepared eels (the fishmonger will do this,
  if preferred)**
Seasoned flour
Salt and pepper
2 egg yolks
2 oz (50 g) breadcrumbs
About 2 oz (50 g) butter for frying
Chopped parsley to garnish

To prepare the eels:

Cut the heads off the eels, and peel off the skin.

Split open the bodies, and remove the backbone and innards.

Wash the fish well in salted water.

Rinse, and dry thoroughly.

To fry the eels:

Cut the eels into 2 inch (5 cm) pieces.

Toss in the seasoned flour.

Beat the egg yolks together.

Dip the eels in the beaten egg, and coat with breadcrumbs.

Heat the butter in a frying pan until very hot.

Fry the eel pieces until crisp and brown.

Arrange the eels on a serving dish.

Lightly fry the parsley in the butter, and use to garnish the
dish before serving.

BUTTERED TROUT
WITH ALMONDS

Serves 6

6 trout (about 5-6 oz (150-175 g) each)
Seasoned flour
6 oz (175 g) butter
3 oz (75 g) blanched almonds, cut into slivers
1 small lemon
Slices of lemon for garnish

Clean the trout, leaving the heads on.

Wash and wipe the fish dry.

Coat each one in the seasoned flour.

Heat 4 oz (100 g) butter in a frying pan.

Fry the trout on both sides until tender and golden brown
— about 10 minutes in total.

Drain the fish, and arrange on a serving dish. Keep hot.

Melt the remaining butter in the frying pan, add the almonds
and fry for a few minutes until golden brown on all sides.

Stir the lemon juice into the pan, and pour it with the
almonds over the fish.

Serve garnished with slices of lemon.

AUNT ELLA'S ROAST CHICKEN

Serves 4

FROM CRAYS POND FARM

For the roast chicken:
1 prepared young roasting chicken (with giblets)
  weighing about 3½-4 lbs (1.5 — 1.75 kg)
Bacon and mushroom stuffing
1 lemon
A few rashers of fat bacon
Fat for roasting

For the bacon and mushroom stuffing:
4 oz (100 g) bacon
2 mushrooms
1 oz (25 g) butter
A teaspoon of finely chopped onion
2 oz (50 g) breadcrumbs
A pinch of dried herbs
Salt and pepper
1 egg

For the giblet gravy:
The giblets from the bird
A sachet bouquet garni
1 onion, chopped
Salt and pepper
1 tablespoon flour
Gravy browning, if required

To make the bacon and mushroom stuffing:

Take the rind off the bacon, and chop into small pieces.

Peel and slice the mushrooms.

Melt the butter in a saucepan. Add the onion and fry for a few minutes. Add the mushrooms and bacon and continue frying until soft.

Remove from the heat.

Stir in the breadcrumbs, herbs and seasoning.

Beat the egg and use to bind the stuffing.

To roast the chicken:

Put into the neck cavity as much bacon and mushroom stuffing as the loose skin will cover. Secure with a small skewer.

Cut the lemon into quarters and put in the body cavity.

Cover the breast with the fat bacon rashers.

Heat the fat in a roasting tin.

Put the bird in the tin, and roast in a hot oven for 15 minutes per lb (450 g). Baste occasionally during the cooking time.

Remove the bacon five minutes before the end of cooking time to brown the breast.

To make the giblet gravy:

Wash the giblets and put them in a saucepan with 1 pint (600 ml/ 2½ cups) of cold water.

Add the bouquet garni, onion and seasoning.

Bring to the boil and simmer for at least 1 hour.

When the bird is cooked, pour off the fat from the roasting tin. Stir the flour into the remaining pan juices.

Gradually stir in the strained giblet stock, and add the gravy browning if required.

Bring to the boil and cook for a few minutes, stirring, until the gravy thickens.

Strain again if necessary, and serve in a gravy boat.

Serve the chicken on a dish, accompanied by bacon rolls, chipolata sausages and bread sauce.

Oven: 400°F/200°C Gas Mark 6

GREAT UNCLE JIM'S ROAST
GUINEA FOWL

Serves 2

FROM COXLEASE FARM

Roast Guinea Fowl is traditionally stuffed with a delicious, fruity raisin stuffing, to prevent drying during cooking. Guinea fowls are usually about the same size as a pheasant and have a similar taste. They are in season throughout the year, but are best from February to June. Guinea fowl used to be classed as game birds, but are now reared on farms.

For the raisin stuffing:
2 oz (50 g) seedless raisins
3 oz (75 g) white breadcrumbs
Grated rind and juice of half a lemon
1 oz (25 g) salted butter or soft margarine
1 egg yolk
About 2 tablespoons milk

For the guinea fowl:
1 prepared guinea fowl (choose a young bird)
Raisin stuffing
½ oz (15 g) butter
Salt and pepper
Bacon rashers to cover the breast
Fat for roasting
A little flour
Watercress and seedless green grapes to garnish

For the gravy:
The giblets from the bird
½ pint (300 ml/ 1¼ cups) water
Salt and pepper
1 oz (25 g) flour
1 tablespoon sherry (optional)

To make the raisin stuffing:

Mix the raisins, breadcrumbs, rind and lemon juice together and blend in the fat.

Blend the yolk and milk together, and bind the mixture with the egg and milk to make a soft stuffing.

12

To roast the guinea fowl:

Stuff the bird with raisin stuffing.

Melt the butter, and brush it over the bird. Season.

Cover the breast with the bacon.

Melt the fat in the roasting tin.

Place the bird in the roasting tin and put in a pre-heated hot oven, reducing the heat and roasting in a moderate oven for about 1 hour. Baste frequently.

Remove the bacon for the last 15 minutes of the cooking time to allow the breast to brown.

Dredge a little flour over the bird a few minutes before the end of cooking time, and let it froth nicely.

To make the gravy:

Put the giblets in a saucepan and cover with water.

Season with salt and pepper.

Bring to the boil, and simmer for about 45 minutes to make game stock.

Put the guinea fowl on a serving dish and keep hot.

Pour off most of the fat in the roasting tin.

Stir in the flour to make a roux.

Gradually add the stock and sherry.

Bring to the boil, then simmer, stirring until the sauce thickens. Strain and serve in a sauceboat.

Serve with roast potatoes and peas accompanied by bread sauce, bacon rolls and garnished with watercress and green grapes.

Oven: 400°F/200°C Gas Mark 6
Reduce to: 350°F/180°C Gas Mark 4

PIGEONS IN CIDER

Pigeons were a popular dish in the 16th and 17th century, when they were kept in dovecots at manor houses and abbeys. Now they are classed as game birds.

2 plump pigeons
Salt and pepper
A little flour
1 onion
Butter or oil for frying
½ pint (300 ml/ 1¼ cups) stock
¼ pint (150 ml/ ⅔ cup) cider
1 tablespoon finely chopped parsley
1 tablespoon finely chopped lemon thyme

Sprinkle the pigeons with salt, pepper and flour.

Peel and chop the onion.

Heat the fat in a saucepan and fry the pigeons for a few minutes to seal, and the onions until soft.

Pour on the stock and cider.

Add the chopped parsley and lemon thyme.

Bring to the boil.

Put the lid on the saucepan and simmer gently for about 45 minutes, or until the birds are tender.

ROOK PIE

This dish is served at The Butchers Arms, Sonning Common, as part of the pub's 'Taste of England' dinner series.

The pie is traditionally made with young rooks and can really only be prepared when the birds are culled around May and June. It used to be a popular speciality in farming communities.

24 young rooks
Approximately 1 pint (600 ml/ 2½ cups) rook stock
A little flour for thickening
Salt and pepper
1 lb (450 g) smoked bacon
½ lb (225 g) onions
A little dripping for frying
½ teaspoon chives
½ teaspoon thyme
1 teaspoon pepper
¾ lb (350 g) shortcrust pastry
Beaten egg

Remove the breasts from the birds and put aside.

Make a stock from the remaining carcasses, thicken with flour and season to taste.

Chop the onions and fry in a little dripping until coloured. Add the rook breasts, bacon cut into cubes, herbs, seasoning and stock.

Bring to the boil and simmer for about an hour.

Correct seasoning.

Put meat into a 3 pint pie dish, cover with pastry and brush with beaten egg. Bake in the oven until golden brown.

Oven: 400°F/200°C Gas Mark 6

CASSEROLED RABBIT IN MUSTARD SAUCE

Serves 4

This is a very old method of cooking rabbit. It can be made without wine by doubling the amount of stock.

1 rabbit
Vinegar
4 oz (100 g) streaky bacon or belly pork
4 medium onions
Fat for frying
1 tablespoon flour
¾ pint (450 ml/ 2 cups) stock
¼ pint (150 ml/ ⅔ cup) red wine
1 bouquet garni
Salt and black pepper
1 teaspoon mustard or to taste
2 oz (50 g) cream
1 dessertspoon chopped parsley

Joint the rabbit, and soak overnight in a bowl of salted water with a dash of vinegar in it.

Drain, rinse and dry the rabbit.

Remove the rind, and cut the bacon or pork into pieces.

Peel and slice the onions.

Heat the fat in a flameproof casserole.

Fry the rabbit on all sides until lightly brown.

Remove and keep on one side.

Lightly fry the bacon or pork and onions.

When cooked, remove and keep with the rabbit.

Blend the flour into the fat to make a roux.

Gradually add the stock and wine, stirring.

Bring to the boil and simmer until the sauce thickens.

Add the salt, pepper and mustard.

Add the rabbit, bacon and onions and the bouquet garni.

Simmer gently for about 1 hour or until the rabbit is tender.

When cooked, put the rabbit on a serving dish.

Remove the bouquet garni.

Reduce the sauce by boiling if required.

Remove from the heat and swirl in the cream.

Spoon the sauce over the rabbit and serve sprinkled with the chopped parsley.

FAWLEY BOTTOM FARM RABBIT PIE

This pie was especially popular at harvest time, when the rabbits were easy targets for the gun as they bolted for cover across the stubble fields.

1 rabbit, jointed
½ lb (225 g) bacon or ham
4 oz (100 g) stewing steak (optional)
4 oz (100 g) onions
A little fat for frying
1 oz (25 g) flour
½ pint (300 ml/ 1¼ cups) rabbit or chicken stock
Salt and pepper
½ lb (225 g flaky or puff pastry
Beaten egg

Cut up the ham or bacon into small pieces.

Cut the steak into cubes.

Peel and slice the onions finely.

Melt the fat in a saucepan and fry the rabbit joints together with the steak, ham or bacon and onions until nicely brown.

Stir in the flour and add the stock. Season.

Bring to the boil and simmer gently for 45 minutes.

Remove from the heat and allow to cool.

Remove any bones from the rabbit meat, and cut into small pieces.

Fill a pie dish with the meat and onion.

Pour over the stock.

Roll out the pastry on a floured board to form a lid.

Make a slit in the top for the steam to escape.

Brush the pastry top with beaten egg.

Bake in a hot oven for 15 minutes, then reduce the heat and cook for a further 30 minutes until golden brown.

Oven: 400°F/200°C Gas Mark 6
Reduce to: 375°F/190°C Gas Mark 5

AUNT ELLA'S BAKED RABBIT   Serves 4

FROM CRAYS POND FARM

1 rabbit
A dash of vinegar
Seasoned flour
1 oz (25 g) chopped onion
4 oz (100 g) lard
½ oz (15 g) brown sugar
1 teaspoon made up mustard
Salt and pepper
1 tablespoon vinegar

Joint the rabbit, and soak overnight in a bowl of salted water with a dash of vinegar in it.

Drain, rinse and dry the rabbit.

Coat the rabbit with the seasoned flour.

Place the rabbit joints in a baking tin with the lard.

Mix together the onion, sugar, mustard, seasoning and vinegar, and spread the mixture over the rabbit joints.

Bake in a moderately hot oven for 45 minutes to 1 hour.

Baste frequently during the cooking time.

Arrange the joints on a serving dish.

Serve very hot with gravy made from the pan juices.

Oven: 375°F/190°C Gas Mark 5

JUGGED HARE WITH FORCEMEAT BALLS

Serves 6-8

Jugged Hare has been popular for many centuries. The name of the dish originates from the deep, stoneware jug in which it was cooked. Traditionally, the rich gravy was thickened with the animal's blood, but this is optional. The hare is similar to a rabbit, but larger, and the flesh is darker and richer. Hares are in season from August to February. A young hare is called a leveret.

1 hare, well hung
Seasoned flour
4 rashers of bacon
2 oz (50 g) fat for frying
1 onion
4 cloves
About 1 pint (600 ml/ 2½ cups) brown stock
Salt and pepper
A pinch of mace and dried mixed herbs
1 teaspoon of grated lemon rind
2 oz (50 g) flour
8 oz (225 g) button mushrooms
1 oz (25 g) red currant jelly
A wineglass of port, madeira or red wine
Chopped parsley

For the forcemeat balls:
1 hare's liver
¼ lb (100 g) fine breadcrumbs
2 oz (50 g) suet
The rind and juice of ½ lemon
1 teaspoon of thyme
1 tablespoon of chopped parsley
Salt and pepper
1 beaten egg
Fat for frying

Ask your butcher to skin, clean and joint the hare.

Retain the blood if required, and the liver for the forcemeat balls.

Coat the hare with the seasoned flour.

Remove the rinds and chop up the bacon.

Heat the fat in a frying pan. Fry the joints with the bacon until golden brown on all sides.

Place the joints in a deep casserole, with the bacon.

Peel the onion, stick the cloves in it, and add it to the casserole. Add enough stock to cover the hare.

Season to taste, and add the herbs and grated lemon rind.

Put a lid on the casserole and cook in a moderately hot oven for 2-3 hours until tender.

Add the mushrooms to the casserole 30 minutes before the end of cooking time.

A few minutes before serving, blend the flour with a little cold water (and the blood of the hare if used).

Stir into the casserole with the red currant jelly and the wine. Cook until the gravy thickens, but do not allow to boil.

Remove the onion before serving sprinkled with chopped parsley and forcemeat balls.

To make the forcemeat balls:

Pound or mince the liver.

Add the breadcrumbs, suet, lemon rind and juice, herbs, and seasoning to taste. Bind the mixture with the beaten egg.

Shape the forcemeat into small balls.

Heat the fat in a frying pan, and fry the balls until light brown.

Drain and serve with the jugged hare.

Oven: 350°F/180°C Gas Mark 4

BRAISED VENISON

The ancient market town of Burford, known as 'The Gateway to the Cotswolds' prospered from the striving wool trade of the Middle Ages. It also became an important staging post for coaches bound for London and Wales. King Henry I was fond of carousing in the town's excellent hostelries after a hunting party in nearby Wychwood. It is said that the men of Burford were renowned for their skill in poaching venison from the forest.

Because venison can be rather dry, it is essential to marinate it before cooking.

For the marinade:
½ pint (300 ml/ 1¼ cups) red wine
3 tablespoons oil
1 teaspoon allspice
1 bay leaf

For the braised venison:
2 lbs (900 g) venison meat, well hung — as the meat is to be braised, it need not be the best cut
1 large onion
1 shallot
2 carrots
½ lb (225 g) streaky bacon
3 oz (75 g) butter or oil for frying
1 sachet bouquet garni
½ pint (300 ml/ 1¼ cups) brown stock
The juice of an orange
1 tablespoon red currant jelly
1 tablespoon cornflour
1 tablespoon milk

To make the marinade:

Mix all the ingredients together in a large bowl, and allow to stand for about an hour before use.

To make the braised venison:

Cover the meat with the marinade and leave for 2 or 3 days if possible, but at least 8 hours, turning occasionally.

Remove the meat and wipe it dry, retaining the marinade.

Peel and chop the onion, shallot and carrots.

Remove the rind and chop the bacon.

Melt the butter or oil in a frying pan, and fry the bacon, onion and shallot until soft.

Put the bacon, onion, shallot and carrot in a casserole dish.

Fry the joint in the hot fat to seal on all sides.

Lay the venison on top of the bacon and vegetables.

Add the bouquet garni, marinade and the stock.

Put the lid tightly on the casserole.

Cook in a moderate oven for 2 hours, or until tender.

Take the venison out of the casserole.

Carve into slices and arrange on a serving dish. Keep hot.

Strain off the gravy from the casserole into a saucepan.

Boil the gravy rapidly to reduce a little, then lower the heat to simmer.

Add the orange juice and red currant jelly, and stir until dissolved.

Mix the cornflour to a smooth paste with the milk.

Stir the cornflour into the sauce.

Bring to the boil and cook, stirring, until the sauce thickens.

Spoon some of the sauce over the venison.

Serve the rest in a sauce boat.

Oven: 350°F/180°C Gas Mark 4

How to Boil a Haunch of Venison

On the night of May 13th 1649 during the Civil War, Oliver Cromwell led six Roundhead regiments through Burford. They surprised a band of Army mutineers — members of an extremist party-known as the Levellers, who considered Cromwell's policies too aristocratic, and had staged a revolt against him. Oliver Cromwell and his men imprisoned 350 of them in the church, one of the finest parish churches in the county, and shot three of the ring-leaders. The bullet holes can still be seen in the stonework, and the carved inscription 'Anthony Sedley, prisner, 1649'.

This dish was favoured by Oliver Cromwell's wife, Elizabeth.

'First stuff your venison with a handful of sweet herbs and parsley minced with a little beef suet and yolks of eggs boiled hard, season your stuffing with pepper, nutmeg, ginger and salt, put your haunch of venison a-boiling, being powdered (with salt) before, then boil up three or four cauliflowers in strong broth and a little milk; when they are boiled, put them forth into a pipkin (saucepan), add to them drawn butter and keep them warm by the fire, then boil up two or three handfuls of spinach in the same liquor, when it is boiled up pour out part of your broth and put in a little vinegar, a ladleful of sweet butter (plain, without salt), and grated nutmeg; your dish being ready with sippets in the bottom, put on the spinach round towards your dish side, then take up the venison being boiled and put it in the middle of your dish and put in your cauliflowers all over it, pour on your sweet butter over your cauliflowers and garnish it with barberries, and the brims of the dish with some green parsley minced. Cabbage is as good done in the same manner as cauliflowers.'

OXFORD JOHN

This regional speciality is served at The Butchers Arms, Sonning Common, which is well known for its good cooking.

This is an easily prepared, herb and lemon flavoured dish and should ideally be made with mutton, but lamb is an acceptable alternative.

About 4½ lbs (2 kg) leg of mutton
6 oz (175 g) shallots
2 oz (50 g) flour
4 oz (100 g) butter
1 lemon
1 pint (600 ml/ 2½ cups) brown stock
1 teaspoon of mixed mace, thyme and parsley
Salt and pepper to taste
Bread croutons

Bone the leg of mutton and cut into slices — about 3 oz (75 g) each.

Finely chop the shallots.

Mix them with the herbs and seasonings and bind with a little of the butter.

Coat the lamb slices with this mixture.

Fry the lamb in the remaining butter for about 10 minutes turning once or twice. Remove the lamb with a slotted spoon.

Stir in the flour and slowly add the stock and the juice of the lemon.

Return the lamb to the pot. Bring to the boil and simmer for 5 to 10 minutes.

Correct the seasoning and serve garnished with bread croutons.

ROAST SADDLE OF LAMB

Serves 10-12

FROM JESUS COLLEGE

The saddle of lamb is a large joint which includes two rumps and two loins. Traditionally Roast Saddle of Welsh Lamb is served at Jesus College, Oxford, on St David's Day, accompanied by roast potatoes and herbs, and served with sautéd leeks and cheese sauce because of the College's Welsh allegiance.

The College's special menu for dinner on that day includes Cream of Chicken and Leek Soup, Grilled Welsh Trout and Lemon, and Welsh Rarebit.

1 saddle of lamb
Fat for roasting
Salt and pepper
3 oz (75 g) brown sugar
2 wineglasses red wine
Brown stock and flour for gravy

Remove the kidneys, and excess skin and fat from the joint.

Fold the sides in, and tie the joint into a neat shape.

Score the fat with a knife, making a diamond pattern.

Melt the cooking fat in a roasting tin, and fry the joint in it to seal.

Season with salt and pepper to taste.

Dredge the joint with the sugar.

Pour the wine into the tin with the joint.

Roast in a hot oven for 20 minutes.

Reduce the heat and continue cooking for the correct time, allowing 20 minutes per lb (450 g) plus an extra 20 minutes.

Baste frequently.

Remove the joint from the oven, and put on a serving dish.

Pour off most of the fat from the roasting tin.

Stir the flour into the remaining fat to make a roux.

Gradually add the stock, still stirring.

Bring to the boil, and simmer until the gravy thickens.

Season to taste and strain.

Serve with the joint in a sauceboat.

Oven: 400°F/200°C Gas Mark 6
Reduce to: 325°F/160°C Gas Mark 3

Lamb

SHEPHERD'S PIE

If beef is used in place of lamb this traditional and popular dish is called Cottage Pie.

For the pie filling:
1 lb (450 g) minced lamb (fresh or left-over)
1 medium onion
Oil for frying
1 oz (25 g) flour
About 5 fl. oz (150 ml/ ⅔ cup) brown stock
1 tablespoon chopped parsley
1 tablespoon tomato sauce
Salt and pepper to taste
2 oz (50 g) grated cheese (optional)

For the potato topping:
1 lb (450 g) potatoes
2 oz (50 g) butter
2 tablespoons milk or cream
Salt and pepper

To make the potato topping:

Peel and cut up the potatoes.

Boil until tender.

Mash well mixing in the butter, milk and seasoning.

To make the shepherd's pie:

Peel and chop the onion.

Heat the oil in a frying pan.

Fry the onion and meat (if using leftover meat, only fry the onion).

Stir in the flour, and gradually add enough stock to moisten nicely.

Stir in the parsley, tomato sauce and seasoning to taste.

Put the meat mixture into an ovenproof dish.

Cover with the creamed potato, marking the top into a pattern with a fork.

Bake in a moderate oven for 30 minutes.

Sprinkle the grated cheese on the top of the pie.

Put the pie under a slow grill to brown the top.

Oven: 375°/190°C Gas Mark 5

OXFORD BEEF STEW

Serves 3-4

1 lb (450 g) stewing or shin of beef
A little flour
2 onions
3 or 4 rashers of bacon
Oil for frying
2 carrots
1 orange
1 teaspoon brown sugar
2 teaspoons vinegar
½ pint (300 ml/ 1¼ cups) beef stock
Salt and pepper to taste

Cut the beef up into cubes.

Roll the meat in the flour.

Peel and chop the onions.

Remove the rind from the bacon, and dice.

Heat a little oil in a saucepan.

Lightly fry the beef, onions and bacon to brown evenly.

Peel and chop the carrots.

Grate the orange rind.

Add the carrots, orange rind, sugar, vinegar, stock and seasoning to the saucepan.

Bring to the boil, then cover and simmer gently for 1½-2 hours.

Alternatively place the stew in a casserole, cover and cook in a moderate oven for the same length of time.

Oven: 350°/180°C Gas Mark 4

OXFORDSHIRE BACON ROLYPOLY PUDDING

Serves 3-4

6 oz (175 g) flour
3 oz (75 g) suet, chopped
A pinch of salt
Water to mix
8 rashers of bacon
2 onions
1 teaspoon chopped sage
2 teaspoons chopped parsley
Pepper

Mix the flour, suet and salt with sufficient water to make a stiff dough.

Roll out on a floured board to an oblong shape.

Remove the rinds from the bacon.

Lay the rashers in rows across the pastry.

Peel and chop the onion.

Cover the bacon with the onion.

Sprinkle with the chopped sage and parsley.

Season with pepper to taste.

Roll up the pastry to form a roll.

Dampen the edges with water and press firmly together.

Put the roll into a well floured cloth and fasten securely.

Put the roll into a saucepan of boiling water.

Reduce to a simmer, cover the pan and cook for 1½ hours, taking care to top up the water as necessary.

STUFFED LOIN OF PORK

Serves 4

For the stuffed loin of pork:
2 lb (900 g) loin of pork, boned
Sage and onion stuffing
Salt and pepper
The juice and grated rind of 1 orange
½ pint (300 ml/ 1¼ cups) cider
A little flour
Watercress to garnish

For the sage and onion stuffing:
1 onion
3 oz (75 g) white breadcrumbs
1 oz (25 g) shredded suet
½ teaspoon finely chopped sage
A pinch of salt and pepper
1 oz (25 g) stoned raisins
1 egg
A little stock, if required

To make the sage and onion stuffing:

Peel and chop the onion and cook in a very little water until soft.

Drain and mix with the breadcrumbs, suet, sage, seasoning and raisins.

Beat the egg and use to bind the mixture to form a stuffing consistency. If more liquid is required stir in a little stock.

To make the stuffed loin of pork:

Finely score the skin of the pork.

Make a slit with a knife to form a pocket between the skin and the meat.

Put the stuffing in the pocket.

Season the underside of the joint with seasoning and sprinkle on the orange rind.

Roll the joint up and tie with string.

Put the joint in an ovenproof casserole.

Add the cider and orange juice, and cover the casserole with a lid or foil.

Bake for 1½ hours at the lower temperature.

Remove the lid, and continue cooking for 30 minutes at the higher temperature to crisp the skin.

Remove the joint from the casserole, and put on a serving dish. Keep hot.

Skim any fat from the pan juices, and use them to make gravy thickened with flour.

Remove the string before serving the joint garnished with watercress.

Serve with the gravy in a separate boat and apple sauce.

Oven: 375°F/190°C Gas Mark 5
Increase to: 425°F/220°C Gas Mark 7

OXFORD SAUSAGES

Makes about 12

Oxford Sausages have been a favourite recipe in the county since the 18th century. They are made from equal quantities of minced veal and pork. The mixture is not put into sausage skins, but is shaped by hand.

12 oz (350 g) veal
12 oz (350 g) pork
4 oz (100 g) shredded beef suet
6 oz (175 g) white breadcrumbs
1 small onion
Grated rind of ½ lemon
½ a grated nutmeg
½ teaspoon sage
½ teaspoon thyme
½ teaspoon marjoram
Salt and pepper
2 egg yolks
A little milk if required
Seasoned flour
Fat for frying

Mince the veal and pork (your butcher will do this if you prefer).

Mix the meat with the shredded suet and breadcrumbs.

Peel and chop the onion finely, and add this to the mixture, together with the lemon rind, nutmeg, herbs and seasoning.

Mix all the ingredients together thoroughly.

Beat the egg yolks and use to bind the mixture to a soft but firm consistency.

If required, add a little milk.

Take a quantity of the mixture (about 1 tablespoonful) and roll it into a sausage shape with the hands.

Roll in the seasoned flour.

Continue until all the mixture has been made into sausages.

Heat the fat in a frying pan, and fry the sausages for 10-15 minutes, turning them during cooking, until golden brown.

FAGGOTS

Faggots are believed to date back to Roman times. The recipe was a useful way to use up left-overs after a pig was killed. Many families had a pig killed once or twice a year.

1 lb (450 g) pig's fry
1 teacup breadcrumbs
2 small onions
5 or 6 sage leaves
A teaspoon salt and pepper
A little flour

Cut the fry (excepting the caul) into small pieces.

Mix all well together.

Put into small heaps.

Wrap them with the caul and place in a tin.

Sprinkle flour on them.

Bake for about ¾ of an hour until brown.

Oven: 400°F/200°C Gas Mark 6

PORK AND BEANS

Serves 4

This dish has been known for centuries. It used to play an important part in country people's diets during the winter. Before the days of refrigeration, meat was salted, pickled or smoked and vegetables dried for storage.

8 oz (225 g) haricot beans
1 lb (450 g) lean pork
2 onions
4 oz (100 g) carrots
1 teaspoon mixed dried herbs
Salt and pepper
1 pint (600 ml/ 2½ cups) stock
2 oz (50 g) flour

Soak the beans in cold water overnight.

Drain, and put the beans in a saucepan with fresh water.

Bring to the boil and simmer for 10-15 minutes, then drain again.

Cut the pork up into small pieces.

Peel and slice the onions and carrots.

Put the meat and vegetables into a casserole.

Add the herbs, seasoning and the stock thickened with the flour.

Cover the casserole and cook in a moderate oven for 1½-2 hours.

Oven: 325°F/160°C Gas Mark 3

COTSWOLD CHEESE DUMPLINGS   Serves 4

2 oz (50 g) cheese
1 oz (25 g) butter or margarine
1 egg
Salt and pepper
2 oz (50 g) finely grated breadcrumbs
1 oz (25 g) golden breadcrumbs
Fat or oil for frying

Grate the cheese finely.

Beat the butter or margarine until creamy.

Beat the egg.

Mix the grated cheese and creamed fat together.

Add the beaten egg, salt and pepper to taste.

Mix with enough finely grated breadcrumbs to form a stiff dough.

Turn the dough onto a floured board.

Form the dough into small balls.

Roll the dumplings in the golden breadcrumbs.

Fry in hot fat until golden brown.

If preferred, the dumplings may be dropped into soup or stew 10-15 minutes before the end of the cooking time. If this method is chosen, do not roll the dough in golden breadcrumbs.

CREAM CHEESE

This recipe is in a letter addressed to General Hendall, of Bury Street, St. James's, London, among the Dillon Family papers dating from the 19th century.

'Put a pint of the best cream in a vessell by itself until it is curdled and pretty firm. Spread the muslin in the basket and with a silver spoon put a little of the cream in the bottom and a little salt over, continuing to do so until the basket is full, let it stand till next day then it must be turned into an other basket with a clean muslin under, and so on till it is sufficiently firm to keep its form when turn'd out on a plate.

The muslin must be coarse and thin.'

PARSNIPS IN CREAM SAUCE
Serves 4

Parsnips have been grown and eaten for centuries. They are still traditionally served with roast beef.

1 lb (450 g) parsnips
½ pint (300 ml/ 1¼ cups) milk
1 oz (25 g) butter or margarine
1 oz (25 g) flour
1 egg yolk
1 tablespoon cream
The juice of half a lemon
Nutmeg or chopped parsley to garnish

Peel the parsnips thinly and cut into quarters lengthways.

Put them in a saucepan of boiling water with enough water to cover, and simmer for about 20 minutes or until tender.

Drain well.

Melt the butter or margarine in a saucepan.

Stir in the flour to make a roux.

Gradually add the milk, stirring.

Bring to the boil, and simmer, still stirring, until the sauce thickens.

Beat the egg yolk with the cream.

Remove the white sauce from the heat, and add the egg and cream mixture. Mix well.

Add the lemon juice gradually.

Toss the parsnips in the sauce.

Return to the heat to make hot, but do not allow to boil again.

Serve in a vegetable dish sprinkled with a little nutmeg or chopped parsley.

THICK POTATO CAKES

Potatoes were first introduced into this country from America in the 16th century.

1 lb (450 g) potatoes
1 oz (25 g) butter
Salt and pepper
About 3 oz (75 g) flour
Fat for frying

Peel the potatoes, and cut in half.

Boil, drain and mash whilst still hot.

Add the butter.

Season with salt and pepper to taste.

Stir in as much flour as the potatoes will absorb without becoming dry.

Spread the rest of the flour on a board.

Turn the potato mixture out onto the board, and knead lightly.

Shape the potato dough into a roll.

Cut into slices about ½ inch (1 cm) thick.

Dust the cakes with the flour.

Cook in hot fat in a frying pan for about 10 minutes until golden brown on both sides.

Serve hot.

These cakes can be made from cold mashed potatoes, but they will not be so light as when made from hot freshly boiled ones.

CARROT PUDDING

8 oz (225 g) carrots
A little salt
4 oz (100 g) butter or margarine
4 oz (100 g) caster sugar
2 eggs
8 oz (225 g) breadcrumbs
1 teaspoon cinnamon
A small pinch of nutmeg

Wash the carrots.

Put them in a saucepan of boiling salted water.

Cook until tender, and drain.

Rub the carrots through a sieve or liquidize in a blender.

Cream the butter and sugar together in a basin.

Separate the eggs.

Beat the yolks into the mixture.

Stir in the breadcrumbs.

Add the carrot purée, cinnamon and nutmeg.

Whisk the egg whites until dry and forming peaks.

Fold the egg whites into the mixture.

Pour into a buttered pudding basin.

Tie down with a cloth or cover with a foil lid.

Steam the pudding for about 2 hours.

Turn out and serve.

DEDDINGTON PUDDING PIE

Serves 4

Called Pudding Pies, these pies were traditionally sold at the village's annual fair. The village, first founded by the Saxons who called it Daedintun, has a long history. Sir Thomas Pope, the founder of Trinity College, Oxford, who was born there in 1508, had the sad duty of telling his friend, Sir Thomas More, imprisoned in the Tower of London, that he was to be executed the following day. Charles I who made his headquarters in Oxford during the Civil War, spent the night at Castle House after his victory over the Roundheads at Cropredy Bridge in 1644.

8 oz (225 g) shortcrust pastry
1 pint (600 ml/ 2½ cups) milk
2 oz (50 g) caster sugar
3 oz (75 g) ground rice
2 oz (50 g) butter or margarine
3 eggs, beaten
½ teaspoon vanilla essence
Candied peel and currants for decoration

Line an 8 inch (20 cm) pie dish with the pastry or cut into rounds and use to line individual patty tins.

Retain a little of the milk.

Heat the rest in a saucepan with the sugar.

Mix the ground rice with the cold milk to a smooth cream.

Stir the rice into the hot milk.

Bring to the boil, and cook gently, stirring until the mixture thickens.

Continue cooking for a few minutes.

Remove the saucepan from the heat.

Stir in the butter, well beaten eggs, and the vanilla essence.

Fill the large or individual pies with the mixture.

Bake in a moderate oven for about 15 minutes, then reduce the heat and continue cooking for a further 30 minutes.

Decorate with thin slices of candied peel and a few currants before serving.

Oven: 350°F/180°C Gas Mark 4
Reduce to: 325°F/160°C Gas Mark 3

APPLE SLICE WITH
CHRIST CHURCH CREAM

Serves 18

FROM CHRIST CHURCH COLLEGE

Christ Church which is known as The House, was founded in 1525 by the Cardinal Wolsey. The college is one of the biggest in Europe with a magnificent Hall, 115 feet long, 40 feet wide and 50 feet high. It has an oak carved hammer beam roof, richly decorated with heraldic badges. Next to the Hall is the Great Kitchen. With its transformed windows and great fireplaces, it remains much as it was when first built by Wolsey. Here can be seen the Cardinal's table, an orginal cooking pit and massive chopping block, cut from a tree trunk that was already 400 years old in Tudor times.

Christ Church Cream is a modern dish, low in fat which was introduced a few years ago and has proved popular, especially when served with Apple Slice.

For the Apple Slice:
2 lbs (900 g) cooking apples (peeled, cored and sliced)
1 soft crust of bread and 2 slices white bread grated into
   fresh breadcrumbs
The juice of 2 lemons
2 teaspoons ground cinnamon
2 tablespoons currants
2 tablespoons sultanas
3-4 tablespoons demerara sugar
Rich shortcrust pastry
Icing sugar for dusting

For the Rich Shortcrust Pastry:
13½ oz (390 g) plain flour
A good pinch of salt
8¾ oz (250 g) butter
3 rounded tablespoons sugar
2 egg yolks
Cold milk

For the Christ Church Cream
2 parts cold custard (egg or proprietary)
1 part natural yoghurt
Caster sugar to taste
A few drops of vanilla essence to taste

44

To make the Rich Shortcrust Pastry:

Sift the flour and salt into a large glass bowl.

Cube the butter into the flour and mix in lightly with the hands.

Stir in the sugar.

Separate the eggs and place the yolks in a measuring jug.

Set aside the whites for use in another recipe.

Pour sufficient cold milk into the measuring jug so that the fluid (including the egg yolks) totals 4 fluid ounces (6 tablespoons / ½ cup).

Beat this with a fork.

Add to the pastry and stir with a metal spoon to bind.

Turn out onto a marble slab, or pastry board.

Knead very lightly and dust with flour.

Wrap in greaseproof paper and chill until required.

To make the Apple Slice:

Place the apple slices in a large bowl.

Pour over the lemon juice and add the breadcrumbs and other ingredients.

Stir to mix well.

Divide the chilled pastry into three equal amounts.

Grease three baking sheets.

Roll each third of pastry into an even rectangle just smaller than the baking sheet and lay carefully onto the sheet.

Pile apple mixture along the centre and fold over the edges to form a strudel effect.

Chill slightly then bake in a warm oven for about 25 minutes until golden brown.

To make the Christ Church Cream:

Combine the cold custard with the natural yoghurt.

Stir in the caster sugar and vanilla essence to taste.

To serve:

Dust the edges only of the apple slice liberally with the icing sugar.

Trim off the ends and cut into even slices.

Serve with Christ Church Cream.

Oven: 350°F/180°C Gas Mark 4

NEW COLLEGE PUDDING or OXFORD DUMPLINGS

Serves 4-6

These small, sweet suet dumplings have traditionally been served at New College, Oxford since the early 19th Century. In the 1820's they were also known in the county as Oxford Dumplings.

4 oz (100 g) shredded suet
A pinch of salt
2 oz (50 g) finely grated breadcrumbs
2 oz (50 g) self-raising flour, sieved
2 oz (50 g) caster sugar
4 oz (100 g) currants
2 oz (50 g) candied peel
2 eggs
1 tablespoon brandy (optional)
A little milk to mix
About 3 oz (75 g) butter for frying
A little caster sugar for dusting

Mix the suet, salt, breadcrumbs, sieved flour and caster sugar together.

Stir in the currants.

Beat the eggs and stir in the brandy.

Stir the egg mixture into the dry ingredients.

Mix to a soft, dropping consistency, adding a little milk if required.

Melt the butter in a frying pan and fry spoonfuls of the pudding mixture until golden brown on both sides.

Sprinkle each pudding with caster sugar before serving hot, accompanied by a sweet sauce.

ICED CARAMEL SOUFFLE   Makes 6 portions

FROM ST. JOHN'S COLLEGE

This soufflé has been devised for this book by Mr. Graham Bayley, the Senior Common Room Chef of St. John's College, to be served in Hall. The College was founded by Sir Thomas White in 1555 on the ruins of the former St. Bernard's College for Cistercian monks. Sir Thomas was a Reading grammar school boy who became a wealthy clothier and Lord Mayor of London. He received Mary Queen of Scots and King Philip of Spain at the Mansion House in London, and also sat on the commission that tried Lady Jane Grey. Over the centuries St. John's has educated countless famous scholars and received many important guests, all of whom have eaten in Hall, which dates from Tudor times.

4 egg yolks
4 egg whites
1 oz (25 g) caster sugar
7 fl. oz (200 ml/ ¾ cup) whipping cream — lightly
**   whisked and well chilled**
3 fl. oz (4½ tablespoons) brandy (optional)
The grated zest of 2 oranges
9 oz (250 g) cubed sugar
3 fl. oz (4½ tablespoons) water
The juice of half a lemon
Finely crushed roasted hazelnuts

Place the cube sugar, water and lemon juice in a heavy saucepan and cook, stirring occasionally until light brown in colour.

Place the egg yolks in a bowl with 2 tablespoons of cold water and whisk for 6-8 minutes until light and frothy.

Add the orange zest and whisk for a further 2 minutes.

When the caramel is ready, remove from heat and add the brandy, if using.

Swirl the saucepan to maintain an even colour until the mixture stops bubbling.

Add the caramel to the egg yolk mixture very slowly, whisking continuously.

Allow to cool, then add the cream.

Whisk the egg whites until slightly peaked.

Add the caster sugar to the egg whites and whisk until stiff.

Fold into the egg yolk mixture.

Place into individual soufflé dishes with collars made from foil.

Put in freezer for 4-6 hours.

Remove collars and roll edges in finely crushed, roasted hazelnuts before serving.

PHOENIX BOMBE

Serves 8-10

FROM BRASENOSE COLLEGE

Brasenose College was founded in 1509 on the former ancient Brasenose Hall. The original brazen nose, from which it gets its name, is a closing or sanctuary ring dating from the 12th-13th century and is preserved in the existing College Hall. There is also a 15th century bronze mask brasen nose on the door of the old gatehouse.

This recipe for Phoenix Bombe has been passed down by the College Chefs over the years. Its origins are not known, but as the College has a Dining Club called the Phoenix, it is believed to have been first produced for the Club. The Phoenix Club is the oldest dining club in Oxford — over 200 years old.

1 pint (600 ml/ 2½ cups) double cream
¾ pint (450 ml/ 2 cups) milk
6 oz (175 g) caster sugar
6 egg yolks
3 oz (75 g) dark chocolate
1 tablespoon concentrated dilute coffee or essence
3 oz (75 g) pistachio (toasted and crushed)
1 tablespoon rum
Chocolate squares, coffee beans and cream to decorate

Whip the yolks and sugar until white.

Meanwhile, heat ½ pint (300 ml/ 1¼ cups) of the cream (reserving the remainder) and all of the milk until almost boiling.

Add the liquid to the yolk mixture and heat until it coats the back of a spoon.

Melt the chocolate in a dish in a very low oven.

Whip the remaining cream to ribbon stage.

Divide the egg mixture into two.

Add the melted chocolate, rum and the pistachios to one half.

Stir until cold, then fold in ¼ pint (150 ml/ ⅔ cup) of the remaining whipped cream.

Flavour the remaining egg mixture with the coffee/essence and fold in the other ¼ pint (150 ml/ ⅔ cup) cream.

Freeze both mixes down, occasionally mixing whilst freezing.

Place two bombe moulds in the freezer.

Remove the coffee mixture from the freezer and use to line the moulds all around. Freeze.

When the coffee lining is hard, fill the centre with the chocolate/rum mixture.

Freeze.

Unmould and divide the portions if required.

Decorate with chocolate squares, coffee beans and cream.

ALADDIN'S CHRISTMAS PUDDING Serves 3

5 oz (150 g) flour
4 oz (100 g) finely chopped beef suet
1 dessertspoon dark brown 'moist' sugar
1 teaspoon bicarbonate of soda
A pinch of salt
1 teaspoon raspberry jam
1 teacup milk

Mix all the dry ingredients together thoroughly.

Then add the raspberry jam and milk.

Pour the mixture into a greased basin dusted with sugar, leaving room for the pudding to rise.

Place a buttered paper on top of the pudding.

Tie down with a cloth and steam for three hours.

Pudding

BROWN BESS

From the recipe book of Lydia Clapton, started before her marriage on 13th March 1918 to Albert Barnes, a baker and grocer in Brize Norton. Their daughter, Kathleen Timms, remembers it was a good, cheap, warming pudding for the winter months, and a good way to use up stale bread. It was also served by her grandfather, also a local bakers.

1 lb (450 g) scraps of bread
3 tablespoons mincemeat
1 egg
3 fl. oz (4½ tablespoons) milk
A little dripping
A little brown sugar

Soak the scraps of bread in cold water for 1 hour.

Squeeze as dry as possible and beat up with a fork.

Mix into them three good tablespoons of mincemeat, 1 egg and 3 fl. oz or ½ teacup of milk.

Grease a pie dish with dripping and put in the mixture.

Sprinkle brown sugar on top.

Bake in a brisk oven till well browned.

Serve very hot.

Oven: 375°F/190°C Gas Mark 5

AUNT TINY'S
CHRISTMAS PUDDING

Serves 4-6

This Christmas Pudding improves with keeping, and is best made a month before Christmas.

4 oz (100 g) soft brown sugar
4 oz (100 g) finely chopped suet
4 oz (100 g) sultanas
4 oz (100 g) raisins
4 oz (100 g) currants
4 oz (100 g) flour
4 oz (100 g) breadcrumbs
2 oz (50 g) candied peel
Grated rind and juice of one lemon
½ teaspoon of mixed spice
Pinch of salt
2 eggs
½ wineglass brandy
A little milk

Mix the dry ingredients together well, adding the grated lemon rind and lemon juice.

Beat the eggs and mix in the brandy.

Add the egg mixture to the dry ingredients and mix well with enough milk to give a soft dropping consistency.

Cover the mixture with a cloth and leave overnight.

Grease a 2 pint pudding basin.

Stir the mixture and put it into the basin. Cover with greaseproof paper, and tie down with a cloth or foil lid.

Steam the pudding in a saucepan of boiling water for 5 hours.

Remove from saucepan and allow to cool. Leave the greaseproof paper but re-cover with a fresh cloth or foil lid. Store in a cool, dry, airy place until required.

On Christmas Day steam the pudding for a further 2-3 hours.

Serve with brandy butter or a sweet white sauce flavoured with rum.

APPLE GINGER

Serves 4

2 lbs (900 g) cooking apples
White sugar
Water
2½ oz (65 g) ginger
A little cochineal

Peel, core and slice the apples, and throw them into cold water.

Take the weight of the apples in the white sugar and ½ pint (300 ml/ 1¼ cups) of water to each 1 lb (450 g) sugar.

Put the water and sugar into a saucepan and, when boiling, add the apples and the ginger.

Simmer gently until transparent.

Colour the syrup with cochineal.

Serve cold with custard.

OXFORD AND CAMBRIDGE PUDDING

Serves 4

12 oz (350 g) apricots
4 oz (100 g) caster sugar
2 eggs
2 tablespoons double cream
6 oz (175 g) shortcrust pastry

Put the apricots in a saucepan.

Cook in a very little water with half the sugar until soft.

Remove the apricot skins and the stones, and chop the fruit up well.

Separate the eggs.

Beat the yolks with the cream, and stir the mixture into the fruit.

Roll out the pastry on a floured board, and use to line a flan dish.

Fill the case with the filling and bake in a moderate oven until set.

Whisk the egg whites until dry and forming peaks.

Fold in the remainder of the sugar.

Pile the meringue on top of the apricot filling.

Make into peaks with a fork.

Bake in a cool oven for a further 20 minutes or until the meringue is golden brown.

Serve hot or cold.

Oven: 350°F/180°C Gas Mark 4
Reduce to: 300°F/150°C Gas Mark 2

GOLDEN PUDDING

Serves 5-6

4 oz (100 g) breadcrumbs
4 oz (100 g) suet
4 oz (100 g) marmalade
4 oz (100 g) sugar
4 eggs

Stir the breadcrumbs with the suet and other ingredients, mixing well.

Beat the eggs well and moisten the pudding with these.

Mix well.

Put into a buttered basin, tie down with a cloth and boil for 2 hours.

When turned out, sift a little sugar on top.

RICE CUSTARD

Serves 3-4

A useful way to use up left-over rice pudding.

2 cups of cold rice pudding
2 eggs
1 oz (25 g) caster sugar

Beat the eggs.

Mix them into the rice pudding with the sugar.

Put into a pie dish and bake for about 45 minutes.

Oven 300°F/150°C Gas Mark 2

CREAMY RICE PUDDING

Serves 4

At the end of the 19th century home-made rice pudding was sold at village shops in Oxfordshire for an old penny a lump. Made in big tins, with milk from local cows, it was cooked on coal-burning ranges until it was solid. Then it was cut up into portions and wrapped in paper.

Traditional versions of rice pudding were flavoured with bay leaves.

2 tablespoons short grain rice
1 pint (600 ml/ 2½ cups) milk
1½ oz (40 g) caster sugar or to taste
1 strip of lemon rind and/or 1 bay leaf (optional)
¼ teaspoonful vanilla essence (optional)
½ oz (15 g) grated nutmeg or cinnamon (optional)
Butter or margarine

Wash the rice and drain.

Put into an oven proof dish.

Add the milk, and stir in the sugar.

Add the chosen flavouring, either strip of lemon rind and/or the bay leaf, stir in the vanilla essence, or sprinkle the nutmeg or cinnamon on top of the pudding.

Dot with butter.

Bake in a slow oven for 2 hours, stirring with a fork after 30 minutes of cooking time.

If used, remove the bay leaf before serving.

Oven: 350°F/150°C Gas Mark 2

PARADISE PUDDING

Serves 5-6

½ lb (225 g) apples
4 oz (100 g) breadcrumbs
4 oz (100 g) currants
4 oz (100 g) sugar
4 eggs
The grated rind of a lemon
A little salt
Nutmeg to taste

Peel, core and chop the apples into small pieces.

Mix the apples with the dry ingredients.

Beat the eggs, and stir them into the mixture.

Put the mixture into a buttered pudding basin.

Tie down with a cloth.

Steam for two hours.

Turn out and serve with a sweet sauce.

BROKEN BISCUIT PIE BASE

At the beginning of this century, broken biscuits were obtained from the big manufacturer, Huntley and Palmers in Reading, and sold in village shops in Oxfordshire. The base makes an attractive and crispy alternative to pastry or sponge.

6 oz (175 g) broken sweet biscuits
3 oz (75 g) butter

Crush the biscuits to a fine mixture. (This is easily done if they are put into a small plastic bag and crushed evenly with a rolling pin).

Melt the butter in a saucepan.

Remove from the heat.

Stir in the crushed biscuits.

Use the mixture to line a greased 8 inch (20 cm) pie dish.

Chill in the refrigerator until set.

POOR MAN'S POUND CAKE

Serves 6-8

This recipe probably gets its name because it is mixed with milk instead of brandy or whisky, as is sometimes used, and which can of course be substituted for the milk if preferred.

4 eggs
8 oz (225 g) caster sugar
8 oz (225 g) butter or margarine
8 oz (225 g) plain flour
1 teaspoon baking powder
8 oz (225 g) mixed peel, grated
1 tablespoon milk (or brandy or whisky if preferred)
1 oz (25 g) walnut halves

Beat the eggs together in a bowl standing in a pan of hot water until thick.

Cream the butter and sugar in another bowl until light and fluffy, and gradually beat in the eggs.

Sieve the flour with the baking powder, and fold it into the mixture.

Mix in the dried fruit and peel.

Stir in the milk, brandy or whisky to give a soft, dropping, batter-like consistency.

Spoon the mixture into a greased and lined square cake tin.

Level the mixture and arrange the walnut halves on top.

Bake in a moderately hot oven for about one hour.

Oven: 375°F/190°C Gas Mark 5

OLD ENGLISH CIDER CAKE
FROM OXFORD

This cake has a distinctive, delicious flavour.

4 oz (100 g) butter or margarine
4 oz (100 g) caster sugar
2 eggs
8 oz (225 g) plain flour
1 teaspoon baking powder or bicarbonate of soda
½ nutmeg
¼ pint (150 ml/ ⅔ cup) cider
Icing sugar for dusting

Cream the butter and sugar together until light and fluffy.

Beat the eggs, in a bowl standing in a pan of hot water, until thick.

Stir the eggs into the mixture.

Sieve the flour with the baking powder or bicarbonate of soda.

Grate the nutmeg finely, and add it into the flour, mixing well.

Stir half the flour into the mixture.

Beat the cider until frothy.

Stir the cider into the cake mixture.

Add the remaining flour.

Mix all together well.

Spoon the mixture into a lined and greased shallow cake tin.

Bake for 45 minutes in a moderate oven, or until golden brown.

Dust the cake with icing sugar when cool.

Oven: 350°F/180°C Gas Mark 4

OXFORDSHIRE LARDY CAKE

Lardy cake is known in various counties with slight variations but it must always be made with pure lard to give the traditional taste. The dried fruit can be either sultanas, currants or raisins, or a mixture of all three.

For the Lardy Cake:
½ oz (15 g) fresh yeast
2 teaspoons sugar
½ pint (300 ml/ 1¼ cups) water
1 lb (450 g) plain flour
2 teaspoons salt
8 oz (225 g) lard
4 oz (100 g) caster sugar
1 teaspoon mixed spice
4 oz (100 g) currants, sultanas or raisins

For the glaze:
1 tablespoon granulated sugar
1 tablespoon water

To make the Lardy cake:

Cream the yeast and sugar with 2 tablespoons of the water, warmed until tepid, to make a paste.

Put in a warm place for approximately 15 minutes, until the mixture becomes frothy.

Sieve the flour and salt into a warmed bowl.

Warm the rest of the water.

Add the yeast mixture and the remainder of the water to the flour, and mix to a dough.

Turn out on to a floured board.

Knead until smooth.

Put into a warm place for approximately 1 hour or until it has doubled in size.

Roll the dough out on a floured board to a rectangular shape.

Cut the lard up into small pats.

If more than one dried fruit is chosen, mix together.

Sprinkle one third of the lard, caster sugar, dried fruit and spice over the dough.

Fold the dough into three, sealing the edges with the rolling pin.

Knead until the ingredients are thoroughly blended.

Repeat this process twice more.

Roll the dough into an oval shape about 1 inch (2.5 cm) thick.

Put on a greased baking sheet and leave in a warm place for 30 minutes.

Bake in a hot oven for 25-30 minutes.

To make the glaze:

When the Lardy Cake is nearly cooked, brush with the glaze, made with one tablespoon sugar and one tablespoon hot water.

Stir the glaze over a gentle heat until the sugar dissolves and forms a syrup.

When removed from the oven, allow the Lardy Cake to cool upside down, so that the lard does not settle at the bottom, but is equally distributed throughout.

Oven: 425°F/220°C Gas Mark 7

BANBURY CAKES

'Ride a cock-horse, to Banbury Cross,
To see a fine lady, upon a white horse,
With rings on her fingers and bells on her toes,
She shall have music wherever she goes.'

The ancient market town of Banbury is famous for this traditional nursery rhyme, and for its cakes. The original Banbury Cross was pulled down in the 17th century. The present cross was built in 1859.

The first record of Banbury Cake-making dates from the 16th century, though they were no doubt made earlier. In medieval days these local specialities were sold hot by street sellers, from round, lidded, wicker baskets. The traditional shape of Banbury Cakes is oval and the filling for them is made from a mince called Banbury Meat.

For the Banbury Meat:
8 oz (225 g) butter
8 oz (225 g) orange and lemon peel, mixed
1 lb (450 g) currants
2 oz (50 g) allspice
½ oz (15 g) cinnamon

For the Banbury Cakes:
1 lb (450 g) puff or flaky pastry
Egg white
Caster sugar for dusting

To make the Banbury Meat:

Cream the butter until light and fluffy.

Chop the orange and lemon peel finely.

Stir the peel, currants, allspice and cinnamon into the butter.

Mix together throughly.

The Banbury Meat can be stored in a covered jar until required.

To make the Banbury Cakes:

Roll out the pastry thinly on a floured board.

Cut into 4 inch (10 cm) ovals (use a paper template for accuracy).

Spread a thin layer of Banbury Meat on half of the pastry ovals.

Moisten the edges with a little water.

Cover with the remaining pastry ovals, pressing the edges firmly together to seal.

Make a slit in each cake for the steam to escape.

Beat the egg white.

Brush the cakes over with the egg white and sprinkle with sugar.

Bake in a hot oven for 15 minutes.

Delicious eaten either hot or cold.

Oven: 425°F/220°C Gas Mark 7

NCC OR NO COOKING CAKE

4 oz (100 g) margarine or butter
2 tablespoons golden syrup
2 tablespoons drinking chocolate
8 oz (225 g) rich tea biscuits, crushed
4 oz (100 g) sultanas
4 oz (100 g) cooking chocolate

Put the fat and the syrup in a bowl.

Stand the bowl in a pan of hot water until the fat and the syrup melt.

Stir in the drinking chocolate, crushed biscuits and sultanas.

Mix well together.

Press the mixture into a greased swiss roll tin.

Melt the cooking chocolate and pour over the cake.

Allow to set before eating this delicious, easy to make, tea time treat.

BAMPTON PLUM CAKE

At Spring Bank Holiday time, a plum cake skewered on a sword is carried through the streets during the traditional Morris dancing, for which the village of Bampton, is famous. The cake is then cut up and sold to bring good luck to all who eat it. Bampton used to be called Bampton in the Bush, as there was no access by road until the middle of the 18th century.

Plum cake was originally made using a rich cake mixture and dried plums, which are of course prunes. Today prunes are not usually used, although the name of this delicious cake lives on.

1 lb (450 g) self-raising flour
8 oz (225 g) butter or margarine
4 oz (100 g) caster sugar
4 oz (100 g) soft brown sugar
1 tablespoon black treacle
8 oz (225 g) stoned raisins
3 eggs
½ teaspoon vanilla essence
Warm milk to mix

Cream the fat, sugar and treacle together until light and fluffy.

Gradually beat in the eggs, one at a time, until the mixture is well blended.

Stir in the dried fruit.

Mix the vanilla essence with the milk.

Sieve the flour, and gradually fold it into the mixture, alternating with a little milk mixture.

Mix to a soft dropping consistency.

Line an 8 inch (20 cm) cake tin with greaseproof paper.

Spoon the mixture into the tin.

Bake in a moderate oven for 2-2½ hours.

Oven: 325°F/160°C Gas Mark 3

SPICED OXFORD CAKE

10 oz (275 g) plain flour
6 oz (175 g) butter
6 oz (175 g) soft brown sugar
½ lb (225 g) raisins
2½ oz (65 g) black treacle
5 fl oz (150 ml/⅔ cups) milk
3 oz (75 g) chopped mixed peel
½ teaspoon mixed spice
¾ teaspoon baking powder

Sift the flour, spice and baking powder.

Rub in the butter.

Add the sugar, raisins and peel.

Mix to dropping consistency with the treacle and milk.

Spoon into a greased 8 inch (20 cm) round cake tin and bake for 1½-2 hours.

Oven: 350°F/180°C Gas Mark 4

GINGERBREAD

When this recipe was written down in the early part of the century by Lydia Clapton, it was noted that the cost was ¼d.

1 lb (450 g) treacle
¼ lb (100 g) brown sugar
¼ lb (100 g) butter
1½ lbs (675 g) flour
1 oz (25 g) ginger
½ oz (15 g) ground allspice
1 teaspoon bicarbonate of soda
¼ pint (150 ml/ ⅔ cup) warm water
3 eggs
1 egg yolk
A little milk

Put the flour in a bowl with the sugar, ginger and allspice.

Warm the butter and add with the treacle to the other ingredients.

Stir well.

Make the water just warm.

Dissolve the bicarbonate of soda in it and mix the whole to a nice, smooth dough with the eggs.

Pour the mixture into buttered tins and bake it for ¾ to 1 hour or longer if thick.

Just before it is done, brush over the top with the yolk of an egg beaten up with milk and finish baking.

Oven: 350°F/180°C Gas Mark 4

MOTHER-IN-LAW'S TEA LOAF

12 oz (350 g) sultanas
4 oz (100 g) demerara sugar
¼ pint (150 ml/ ⅔ cup) strong cold tea
1½ fl. oz sherry
1 egg
2 oz (50 g) walnuts
1 lemon
8 oz (225 g) self-raising flour

Put the sultanas and sugar in a bowl.

Pour on the tea and stir in the sherry.

Leave to infuse overnight.

Shell and chop the walnuts.

Finely grate the lemon rind.

Beat the egg.

Add the flour, walnuts, lemon rind and egg to the mixture.

Beat well.

Put the mixture into a greased 7 x 4 inch (18 cm x 10 cm) loaf tin.

Bake in a moderate oven for 1¼ hours.

Oven: 350°F/180°C Gas Mark 4

WHOLEMEAL BREAD

Makes two 2 lb (900 g) loaves

2 oz (50 g) fresh yeast
1 tablespoon caster sugar
3 lbs (1.5 kg) plain wholemeal flour
2 teaspoons salt
1 oz (25 g) lard
1½ pts (900 ml/ 3¾ cups) warm water

Mix the yeast and sugar with ½ pint (300 ml/ 1¼ cups) of the water, and leave in a warm place for 10 minutes until frothy.

Add the salt to the flour and mix well.

Rub the lard into the flour.

Pour the yeast liquid on to the flour.

Mix well to make a soft dough.

Knead on a floured board until smooth and elastic.

Shape into a ball, and leave in a bowl covered with lightly oiled polythene (to prevent a skin forming) and leave to rise until double in size.

Knead well again until firm.

Grease two 2 lb (900 g) loaf tins.

Divide the dough in two and shape to fit the tins.

Cover the tins with lightly oiled polythene and leave to rise again at room temperature for about one hour, when the dough should have risen almost to the top of the tins.

Bake in a pre-heated hot oven for 35 minutes.

Turn out and cool on a wire rack.

A properly cooked loaf should sound hollow when tapped on the bottom.

Oven: 425°F/220°C Gas Mark 7

GREAT GRANDMOTHER'S
GREENGAGE JAM   Makes about 7 lbs (3.25 kg)

FROM FAWLEY BOTTOM FARM

For a lovely green jam, use fully grown fruit, which is not quite ripe. Jam
made with ripe fruit will be yellow.

4 lbs (1.75 g) greengages
¾ pint (450 ml/ 2 cups) water
4 lbs (1.75 g) preserving sugar

Remove any stalks from the greengages.

Cut the fruit in half and remove the stones.

Tie the stones in a muslin bag.

Put the fruit, stones and water into a preserving pan or large
heavy saucepan.

Cook gently until the greengages are quite soft.

Add the sugar, and stir until it is dissolved.

Increase the heat and bring to the jam to a rolling boil.

Boil rapidly, stirring frequently for about 10 minutes or until
setting point is reached.

Setting point is reached when the temperature tested with
a thermometer reaches around 220°F/105°C or when a little
of the jam put on a cold saucer wrinkles when pushed gently
with a finger.

Remove the muslin bag of stones.

Allow to cool.

Pour into clean, dry 1 lb (450 g) jam jars and cover tightly
with jam covers.

OXFORD MARMALADE   Makes 5 lbs (2.25 kg)

2 lbs (900 g) Seville oranges
4 oz (100 g) lemons
2½ pints (1.4 litres/ 6¼ cups) water
3 lbs (1.4 kg) warmed preserving sugar

Cut the fruit in half.

Remove the pips and tie them in a muslin bag.

Squeeze the juice.

Shred the peel with a knife to the thickness you like.

Put the bag of pips, the juice, peel and water in a bowl, and leave to soak overnight to soften the rind and draw out the pectin as an aid to setting.

Remove the bag of pips.

Put all the ingredients from the bowl into a preserving pan.

Bring to the boil and cook for about one hour or until tender.

In the meantime warm the sugar in a low oven.

When the fruit is tender, stir in the sugar, and boil the mixture rapidly, until the marmalade jellies when a little is tested on a cold saucer.

Allow the marmalade to rest for 15 minutes.

Stir well, and pot.

Cover with purchased jam covers.

BLACK CURRANT CHUTNEY

1 lb (450 g) black currants
1 lb (450 g) dark brown sugar
4 oz (100 g) raisins
1 oz (25 g) mustard seed, crushed
½ oz (15 g) ground ginger
1 oz (25 g) salt
4 oz (100 g) onion
About ½ pint (300 ml/ 1¼ cups) vinegar

Strip the black currants from the stalks.

Stone and chop the raisins.

Peel and chop the onion.

Put the currants in a preserving pan and cover with the vinegar.

Cook gently until the black currants are tender.

Leave to cool.

Stir in the sugar, chopped raisins, mustard seed, ground ginger, salt and onion. Mix well.

Bring to the boil, then cook, stirring occasionally until the chutney becomes thick.

Allow to cool.

Pot and seal securely with jam covers, then with a circle of cloth brushed with melted candle grease to make airtight.

Store in a cool place away from the light.

OXFORD SAUCE

This sauce is excellent served cold with ham, chicken, duck, goose and venison.

The rind of half an orange
½ lb (225 g) red currant jelly
½ teaspoon of made up English mustard
2 tablespoons port
The juice of half a lemon

Peel the rind from the orange.

Blanch the rind for a few minutes in boiling water.

Drain and chop very finely.

Mix the red currant jelly, mustard, port and lemon juice together thoroughly.

Stir in the chopped orange peel.

OXFORD CIDER CUP

Makes about 3½ pints (2 litres / 9 cups)

16 strawberries
Half a cucumber
4 oz (100 g) caster sugar
A little water
1¾ pints (1 litre/ 4¼ cups) champagne cider
1¾ pints (1 litre/ 4¼ cups) soda water
1 wineglass of any liqueur
A pinch of nutmeg
Ice

Wash and hull the strawberries.

Peel the cucumber in strips, and cut it into neat pieces.

Melt the sugar in a little water, and allow it to cool.

Mix the cider, soda water, liqueur, sugar and nutmeg together in a large jug.

Chill.

Add the strawberries and cucumber peel.

Serve as soon as possible with the addition of some table ice.

OXFORD SWEET BISHOP PUNCH

Makes 3 pints (1.75 litres / 6 cups)

Punch first became popular during the 17th century.

6 oz (175 g) lump sugar
4 lemons
2 Seville oranges
24 cloves
1 pint (600 ml/ 2½ cups) water
½ teaspoon allspice
½ teaspoon ground cinnamon
½ teaspoon ground ginger
½ teaspoon ground mace
2 pints (1.15 litres/ 5 cups) port

Rub the sugar on the rind of 2 of the lemons, until the zest is removed.

Squeeze the juice from these 2 lemons.

Put the sugar in a jug and pour the strained lemon juice over it.

Score the rind of the remaining 2 lemons and the 2 oranges.

Stick 6 cloves into each fruit.

Roast the oranges and lemons in a moderately hot oven for about 45 minutes until soft and brown.

Cut the fruit into quarters and put into a large saucepan.

Add the water, spices, port, sugar and lemon juice.

Simmer gently for 30 minutes.

Strain and serve hot.

Oven: 375°F/190°C Gas Mark 5

BROWN BETTY

Makes 3 pints (1.75 litres/ 7½ cups)

An early 19th century hot punch from Oxford.

3 oz (75 g) brown sugar
1 pint (600 ml/ 2½ cups) hot water
1 slice of lemon
Cloves
Cinnamon
Brandy
2 pints (1.15 litres/ 5 cups) strong ale
Brown toast
Nutmeg
Ground ginger

Dissolve the sugar in the water.

Add the lemon slice, cloves, cinnamon and brandy to taste.

Add the ale and heat in a pan, without bringing to the boil.

Serve hot, with a slice of brown toast floating on top of each glass and sprinkled with grated nutmeg and ginger.

Punch Bowl

BRASENOSE ALE or LAMB'S WOOL

Makes 3 pints (1.75 litres/ 6 cups)

Brasenose Ale is served in Hall at Brasenose College after dinner on Shrove Tuesday. The original name for the drink was 'La Masubal', which over the years has become corrupted to Lamb's Wool. The baked apple pulp floating on top of the hot, spiced ale looks rather like a lamb's fleece.

12 small to medium cooking apples
3 pints (1.75 litres/ 6 cups) brown beer or ale
A pinch of nutmeg
A pinch of ground ginger
Sugar to taste

Put the apples on a baking sheet.

Bake in the oven for about 45 minutes until soft.

Remove from the oven, and peel.

Mash the fruit and add to the beer.

Rub through a sieve.

Put into a saucepan, and add the nutmeg, ground ginger and sugar to taste.

Heat through gently, and serve hot.

If preferred, the baked apples may be added whole to the hot spiced ale.

Oven: 375°F/190°C Gas Mark 5

HOMEMADE LEMONADE

Makes 3 pints (1.75 litres/ 6 cups)

3 large lemons
3 tablespoons caster sugar
3 pints (1.75 litres/ 6 cups) water
Slices of lemon to decorate

Wash the lemons.

Peel the rind with a potato peeler to give very fine strips, avoiding cutting any of the white pith.

Put the rind and the sugar in a jug.

Leave to stand for about an hour for the sugar to draw the essential oil from the rind.

Squeeze the juice from the lemons.

Add the juice to the jug with the *cold* water — to preserve the vitamin C.

Stir with a wooden spoon.

If possible, leave in the refrigerator for 24 hours.

Strain before serving with ice cubes, and slices of lemon to decorate.

COCOANUT TOFFE

(This is the spelling as it appears in Lydia Clapton's old recipe book.)

2 oz (50 g) butter
2 lbs (900 g) white sugar
½ teaspoon ground ginger
1 tablespoon vinegar
1 tablespoon desiccated coconut

Put the butter in a saucepan and let it melt.

Add the sugar, ground ginger, vinegar and desiccated coconut.

Stir well and boil for half and hour.

Pour into greased tins.

Sprinkle more coconut over.

Let it stand until cold.

COLOURED AND DECORATED EGGS FOR EASTER

A Synod was held in Burford to decide upon the date of Easter in AD 685. The tradition of decorating hard-boiled eggs on Easter Sunday morning is of great antiquity. Very popular with children, the hard-boiled eggs can be hidden in the house and garden to add to the fun.

Allow 1-2 eggs per person
A pinch of salt

For colouring and decorating the eggs:

Before boiling in coloured water, a child's name or a design can be drawn on each egg by using a candle, sharpened to a point like a pencil. The candle grease prevents the colour taking and so the name or design will stand out well. Alternatively, design, names or funny faces can be painted on the eggs after they have been hard-boiled, using poster paints.

For pink — add plenty of cochineal.

For green — add plenty of green colouring.

For mottled yellow and brown — tie onion skins round the eggs with string.

To boil the eggs:

Bring the water to the boil in a saucepan.

Add the chosen colouring, and a pinch of salt to prevent the shells cracking.

Gently put in the eggs.

Bring back to the boil, then simmer for 3-4 minutes if required soft-boiled, 10-15 minutes for hard-boiled.

Serve soft-boiled eggs at once. Hard-boiled eggs should be plunged into cold water before shelling, to prevent discoloration.

Acknowledgements:

Grateful thanks are extended to the many people of Oxfordshire who have contributed towards this collection of recipes, especially:

Kathleen Timms of Brize Norton for Brown Bess, Faggots, Paradise Pudding, Rice Custard, Golden Pudding, Aladdin's Christmas Pudding, Apple Ginger, and Cocoanut Toffe from her mother's cookery book.

Lawrence Batty of Sevenoaks, Kent, for Aunt Tiny's Christmas Pudding, and information about his family records.

Bob Gallimore, Deputy Editor of the Henley Standard for information.

Leon Banks, Landlord of The Butchers Arms, Sonning Common, for Oxford John and Rook Pie.

Dr. Robert Gasser, Bursar, and Chef, Mr. R. Stafford of Brasenose College, Oxford, for Phoenix Bombe.

John Harris, Steward of Christ Church, Oxford, for Apple Slice with Christ Church Cream.

Commander Simon Stone, the Home Bursar and Richard Barton, Head Chef of Exeter College, Oxford, for Bongo Bongo.

Air Commodore J.G. De 'Ath, the Home Bursar and the Chef, Mr. K. Morgan of Jesus College, Oxford, for Roast Saddle of Lamb.

Nicholas Purcell, the Domestic Bursar and Graham Bayley, Senior Common Room Chef of St. John's College, Oxford, for Iced Caramel Soufflé.

Phyllis Jorden of Huddersfield, for NCC or No Cooking Cake.

The Oxfordshire County Record Office for Cream Cheese from the Dillon Family papers (DIL XXVI).

THE COUNTRY RECIPE SERIES

Available now @ £1.95 each

Cambridgeshire
Cornwall
Cumberland & Westmorland
Devon
Dorset
Hampshire
Kent
Lancashire
Leicestershire
Norfolk
Oxfordshire
Somerset
Suffolk
Sussex
Warwickshire
Yorkshire

All these books are available at your local bookshop or newsagent, or can be ordered direct from the publisher. Just tick the titles you require and fill in the form below. Prices and availability subject to change without notice.

Ravette Books Limited, 3 Glenside Estate, Star Road, Partridge Green, Horsham, West Sussex RH13 8RA.

Please send a cheque or postal order, and allow the following for postage and packing. UK 25p for one book and 10p for each additional book ordered.

Name...

Address..

....

....